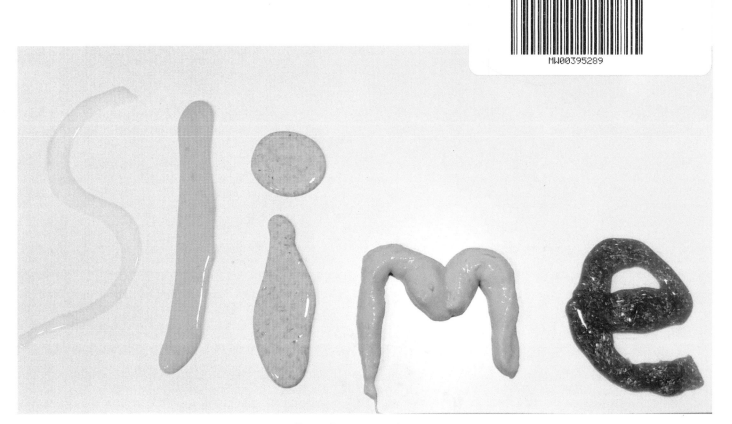

Dedicated to,

My mom and dad for helping me write this book and putting up
with the mess.

2017©STUDIOPENGU

Table of Contents

Introduction

Hi! Welcome to "The Ultimate Guide to Slime". I've been making slime for a couple of years, and I've noticed that there are not many exact recipes for slime. This book is the remedy to that situation.

I enjoy making and playing with slime for stress and anxiety relief. It's entertaining to play with, no matter your age. Just experiment and have fun, that's all that really matters.

Much like cooking, making slime requires a margin of trial and error. As you gain experience, you will be able to modify recipes to suit your liking better. Be patient, my first attempts ended up in the trashcan.

The recipes make 2 – 4 ounces of slime. 2 ounces is about the size of a racquetball, and 4 ounces is a tennis ball. My sizes are by weight, not volume.

Do Not Eat or Allow to be eaten especially by children & pets

Do not pour completed recipes down sink.

Check out my slime account on Instagram @weslime247

Types of Slime

Bubble Blowing Slime – This slime is made for blowing bubbles. It is not good for playing with since it doesn't have a nice texture.

Bubblegum Slime – This slime is super squishy and stretchy. It is spreadable like Butter or Cream Cheese Slime.

Butter Slime – This slime is spreadable and has a matte texture. This slime is very moldable and is great for projects.

Clay Slime – This slime is very thick and can be molded slightly. The slime has a matte finish.

Clear Slime – A clear version of slime. It has a squishy consistency and is great for looking at and placing stuff inside.

Cream Cheese Slime – This slime feels like Butter Slime. This slime is spreadable and is quite moldable.

Floam Slime – This slime has foam beads in it and has a crunchy sound.

Fluffy Slime – A basic slime that has a fluffy and bouncy consistency. Good for swirling and poking. Creates bubbles on top after sitting overnight or longer.

Frosting Slime – a Fluffy Variant that temporary holds shape and is spreadable like Frosting.

Glossy Slime – This slime is like Fluffy Slime, but with a Glossy finish. This slime is a bit more squishy than Fluffy Slime.

Jiggly Slime - A slime made more for poking than squishing. Very squishy and jiggles when you poke it.

Marshmallow Slime – Has a bouncy feel and texture. It is squishy and is shiny when it sits. When played with, it becomes matte.

Oobleck Slime – When stretched, this slime becomes more solid than liquid. When it sits without being touched, it runs like water.

Pearl Slime – This slime feels like a clear slime. It looks like a melted pearl.

Quick Clear Slime – This slime feels more jelly-like than normal Clear Slime. It clears up much faster than the normal Clear Slime.

Soft Serve Slime – This slime is runny and pourable. It feels like Soft Serve Ice cream.

Sonic Slime - This slime feels like a Glossy Slime. This slime has a nice high pitch sound.

Sonic Boom Slime – Feels like its original version, Sonic Slime. It has a lower pitch sound and feels thicker.

Spa Slime – a therapeutic experience for your hands that leaves lotion on your hands when handled.

Taiko Slime – This slime is clear and is jelly-like. This slime sounds like a Taiko Drum when tapped on.

Therapeutic Slime – This slime is great for adults or people who want to use slime for relaxation. It can also be used to rehab tired or sore hands.

Bubble Blown with Slime

Supplies

Clear Glue

White Glue

Food Dye

Scent Oil

White Glue – Glue must be a water based PVA glue to properly work. There should not be a chemical smell to the glue. Standard School Glue works well. It can be sourced from Wal-Mart, Staples, Office Depot, Target, Michaels Craft, Craft Supply Stores, Lakeshore and other Teacher's Supply Stores.

Clear Glue - Glue must be a water based PVA glue to properly work. There should not be a chemical smell to the glue. It can be sourced from Wal-Mart, Staples, Target, Michael's Crafts, Craft Supply Stores, Lakeshore and other Teacher's Supply Stores. There are also online retailers.

Food Flavorings – Our choice for scenting our slime. Used to flavor foods such as candy these Flavorings are Non-Toxic. They can be sourced quite readily from Cake / Candy Supply Stores. Michaels Craft Store and some grocery stores carry them but have a limited selection.

Essential Oils – Can be used to add scents to your slimes. Bed Bath and Beyond, Wal-Mart, Target or Online retailers. Make sure the Oils are non-toxic. Always test on a small bit of slime to assure that the oils do not discolor your slime as some brands use added coloring agents.

Food Coloring – Used to color the slime. Food dyes usually produce a pastel color. Most Grocery Stores, Wal-Mart, Cake / Bakery Supply Stores or Online Retailers carry Food Safe dyes. Can be mixed together to produce multitudes of colors. Make sure to use the liquid form, not the gel form as it will not mix properly.

Paint – Used to color your slime. Paint can produce deeper colors than food dye and comes in more shades than food dyes. Acrylic / Water Based Paints are the best. Oil based paints work but can stain other objects so it should be avoided. Specially paints like Airbrush, Spray Paint etc. should be avoided as they do not mix well. Michaels, Wal-Mart and other Art Supply stores are your best options to find the hues you desire. Can be mixed together to produce multitudes of colors.

Glow-in-the-Dark Paint – Craft Stores usually stock Glow-in-the-Dark Paint. Look for Acrylic / Water Based Paints.

Hand Lotion – Used to create soft slimes or to repair slimes that have toughened. Most lotions will work. Look for varieties with a good and no scent. Additives like Aloe, Shea Butter etc. do not usually affect slimes.

Foaming Hand Soap – Produces a runny, bubbly consistency. Look for a variety that is clear with little or no scent.

Corn Starch – Most Grocery Stores or Bargain Stores will carry corn starch in the Baking Aisle.

Baby Powder – Can be used as a substitute for corn starch Only use brands that contain 100 Percent Corn Starch.

Baby Oil – Used to add shine to slimes.

Soft Clay – Crayola Model Magic is best but other soft clays work. Toys R Us and other big box retailers stock Crayola while discount shops often have other brands.

Shampoo – Natural or Moisturizing Shampoos work the best. We use Suave Almond + Shea butter Moisturizing Shampoo. Should look like a pearl when squeezed out. Most normal shampoos do not work.

Thermochromic Pigments – Used to create color changing slime. Hard to find locally so purchasing from internet sites is advised. Generally, these pigments are quite expensive.

Borax – Used to activate the mixture to turn into slime. Can be purchased at most grocery stores and big-box retailers. If you cannot find it in local stores it can be purchased online. Please check local regulations before importing.

Liquid Laundry Detergent – can be used in place of Borax activator. Should be colorless and unscented unless you want that scent.

Liquid Starch – can be used as an activator. A Better option than detergent as it usually doesn't contain scents or colors.

Glitter – Used to add shimmer to slimes, glitter is a great addition. It can be added to any slime but works best in clear slime. It can even lend color to clear slime. Glitter tends to sink through the slime creating interesting patterns and effects in your creation. We recommended using Extra Fine glitter as it gives the best results, but fine or large glitter will also work.

Beads and Baubles- Craft Stores, Wal-Mart, Toy Stores are great places to find beads and other small objects to sink into slime. Miniature robots make great party favors for birthday parties.

Polystyrene Beads / Foam Beads – Used to create Floam. Michaels, Hobby Lobby, Joanna's fabric are great places to source pillow stuffing beads. Faux snow can also be used and can be sourced around the holidays from various retailers. Travel Pillows are another source for beads. You should be able to feel the beads inside.

Contact Lens / Saline Solution – Can be used as an activator when mixed Baking Soda. Can be purchased at most big box retailers, grocery stores and pharmacies.

Bowls- Dollar Store and other bargain stores carry a wide variety of plastic bowls. Disposable bowls are often not strong enough to mix slime in and should be avoided. If you do use disposable products, choose paper over foam as the foam cracks easily.

Containers – To keep your slime malleable, it must be stored in an airtight container. Plastic containers with locking lids are the best. Soufflé Cups also work well. Plastic bags should be avoided as slime sticks to them making it hard to remove. Discount / Bargain Stores are a great place to get plastic containers. Soufflé Cups can be purchased from restaurant supply stores, party supply stores and some grocery stores.

The Slime of ...

Tools

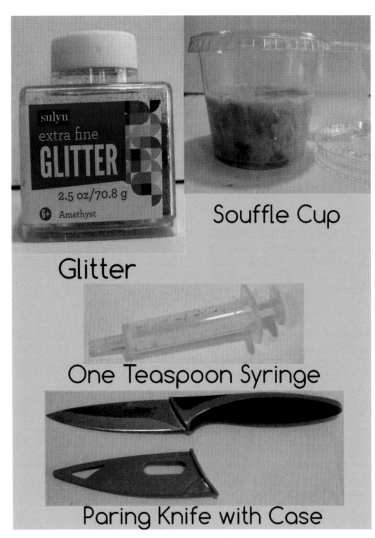

Glitter

Souffle Cup

One Teaspoon Syringe

Paring Knife with Case

Spoons

Spray Bottles – Can be used to store and use different solutions.

Measuring Spoons

Wax Paper – Use to build projects on.

Pizza Cutter – Used in projects to cut slime.

Cookie Cutters – Used in projects to cut slime.

Spatulas – For mixing slime.

One Teaspoon Syringe – one of the most useful tools. It is used to introduce Activator, Scents, Dyes and other solutions into the slime in a controlled fashion

Knives - Get one with a cover for safety.

Most of the tools you'll need can be purchased cheaply at 99 Cents Store, Dollar Tree and other bargain shops. Most grocery stores and big box retailers also carry them. Disposable utensils will also work. Popsicle sticks are another cheap option.

Activators

Our activator recipe is the most universally compatible activator and is also the cheapest. There are other options that we discuss here.

1. **Activator**

   Mix 1 tsp with 1 Cup of Hot Water. Mix until Borax is completely dissolved. Pour in a spray bottle or sealable container.

   When adding to slime, add in ½ increments. You are looking for the slime to pull away from the bowl. There should be little or no liquid glue at the bottom of the bowl.

   Adding too much activator will cause slime to become overly tough and in some recipes, can completely ruin the slime.

2. **Saline Solution / Contact Lens Cleaner / Eye Drops**

   If Borax is unavailable in your area, you can use any of the solutions above as a substitute. These are preferable to Starch or Detergent.

   In a bowl mix 4 Tbsp. of Saline Solution to 1 Tsp of Baking Soda. Use same measurements as normal activator.

   None of these solutions outperform the other and can be interchanged as necessary

3. **Liquid Starch / Laundry Detergent**

   You can also use Liquid Starch or Liquid Laundry Detergent, undiluted at same measurements as normal activator. Liquid Starch is preferable as it contains less aroma and coloring agents than laundry detergent. Laundry Detergents also have various chemical compositions and could affect slime. Natural Laundry Detergent generally performs poorly.

   We recommended using liquid starch over Laundry Detergent.

Coloring and Scenting

For best result mix in scents or dyes before adding activator to the slime.

Colors generally show up better in clear slimes than in slimes made with standard glue.

To add color or scent to previously made slime: roll slime into a ball and make a well in the top. Add a few drops of dying / scenting agent into well and close hole. Stretch and fold slime until agent is completely mixed in. If color or scent is not to your liking, repeat the process. Add Food Dyes and Paint sparsely, as too much will stain your hands.

You can use Nitrile or Latex Examination Gloves like the doctor's use.

1. Food Coloring

Only use liquid based dyes, gel types do not mix well.

Most recipes will take about 1-3 drops.

Multiple colors can be mixed together. Make one color first and then add additional colors.

2. Paints

Used water based acrylic paint for best results.

Most recipes will require 6-8 drops.

Multiple colors can be mixed together. Make one color first and then add additional colors.

Do not use paint in clear slime if you want to retain its translucency.

3. Food Flavorings

Use clear clean scents. Complicated scents such as Cookies and Cream do not translate well when mixed with slime. Bubblegum, Marshmallow, Butter, Mint and Fruity scents such as Lemon really work well.

Most recipes require between 2 to 5 drops but more can be added if desired more can be added as the scent fades.

4. Essential Oils (Topical Use Only)

Do Not Use burning oils as they are not always safe to touch.

Adding Oils such as Lavender or Mint can turn slime into a relaxing squeeze ball.

Most recipes require between 4 to 8 drops but more can be added if desired.

More can be added as the scent fades.

Oils and their Effect

1. Mint – Energizing
2. Lavender – Calming and Relaxing. Great before sleep
3. Lemon – Promotes mental clarity
4. Rose- Balance and Harmony
5. Orange – Uplifting
6. Citrus (Grapefruit, Lime) – Uplifting
7. Jasmine - Tranquility

Fun Scents

1. Bubblegum
2. Cherry
3. Peanut Butter
4. Cake Batter
5. Tutti Frutti
6. Cinnamon

Tips and Techniques

1. Drag Technique – pull stirring utensil slowly towards you to avoid creating bubbles.

2. Kneading – Be sure to thoroughly knead the slime.

3. Don't add too much activator! If you do, follow the Hardening Slime section in Slime First Aid

4. Use a syringe for activator because you can be more precise.

5. Store slime in a cool, dark environment. Extreme heat and cold can alter slime.

6. When Photographing or Video Recording, choose backgrounds that compliment slime

7. Use white backgrounds for darker slimes.

8. Use complementary colors for lighter slimes (White, Baby Pink, etc.)

9. Use natural bushes or flowers for a nice background

10. Make sure your lighting is good before you start photographing or video recording. Natural Light is of course the best.

11. If you have a tripod, use it! Or make one.

A Tripod will free up your hands to play with your slime while filming and provides a steady platform for photographs.

Recipes

All difficulty levels and reviews are opinions. They all depend on your experience, and personal tastes.

Bubble Blowing Slime

This super light slime can be blown into bubbles.

Difficulty: Easy

Review: 3.5 / 5

Supplies:

White Glue

Foaming Hand Soap

Corn Starch

Activator

Directions:

Makes 1 1/2 Ounces

In a bowl add 4 Tbsp. of White Glue to 1 Tbsp. of Foaming Soap

Mix

Add 1-2 Teaspoons of Activator

Mix thoroughly and adjust activator until proper consistency is achieved.

Knead in ½ Tbsp. of Corn Starch

Let stand for 5 -10 Minutes before trying to inflate.

To inflate see Projects Section

Store in an airtight container

Bubblegum Slime

A great slime for stretching and swirling. Very squishy, but it can be sticky.

Difficulty: Medium

Review: 3.5 / 5

Supplies:

Clear or White Glue

Shaving Cream

Corn Starch

Hand Lotion

Foaming Hand Soap

Activator

Scenting Agent (optional)

Glitter (optional)

Directions:

Makes 3 Ounces

In a bowl add 4 Tbsp. of Glue to 1 Tbsp. of Shaving Cream

Mix

Add ¼ Tbsp. of Hand Lotion

Mix

Add 1 Tbsp. Foaming Hand Soap

Mix

Add 1 ½ Tbsp. of Corn Starch

Mix

Add in dying agents, glitter, beads and scent until color and fragrance is to your liking.

Mix

Add 1-2 Teaspoons of Activator

Mix thoroughly and adjust activator until proper consistency is achieved.

Add 1 Tbsp. of Corn Starch

Mix

Store in an airtight container

BubbleGum Slime

Normal

Butter Slime

As the name implies, Butter Slime is a spreadable, moldable and stretchy slime.

Difficulty: Medium

Review: 4.5 / 5

Supplies:

White or Clear Glue

Shaving Cream

Activator (See Solutions for Recipe)

Hand Lotion

Soft Clay

Food Coloring / Paint (Optional)

Scenting Agent (Optional)

Directions: Makes 4 Ounces.

In a Bowl, Mix 7 tbsp. of Shaving Cream to 4 tbsp. of White Glue.

Mix in 1/8 tbsp. of Hand Lotion.

Add 1 tsp of Activator.

Mix thoroughly and adjust activator until proper consistency is achieved.

Add an equal amount of soft clay based on volume.

Knead until thoroughly mixed.

Mix in dying agents, glitter, beads and scent until color and fragrance is to your liking.

Store in Airtight Container.

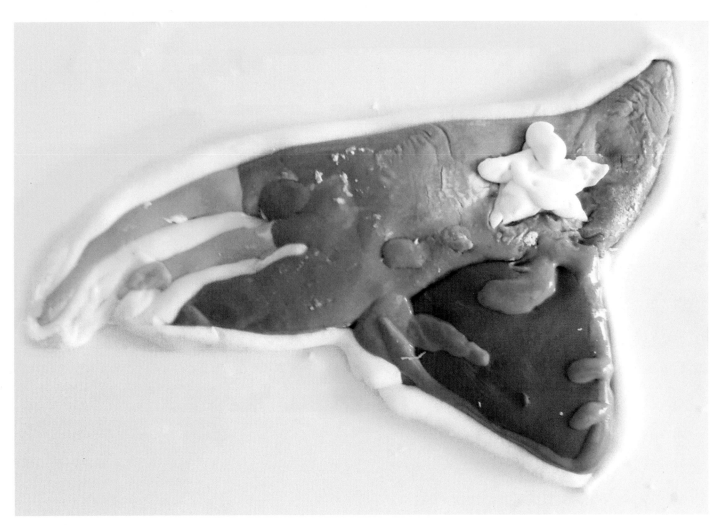

Normal

New England Patriots Logo Created with Butter Slime for Super Bowl 51

Clay Slime

Moldable and very Stretchy, Clay Slime is an excellent all around slime for playing with. It looks sticky, but it removes very easily.

Difficulty: Medium

Review: 5 /5

Supplies:

White or Clear Glue

Corn Starch

Hand Lotion

Activator

Food Dye or Paint (optional)

Scenting Agent (optional)

Directions: Makes 4 1/2 Ounces

In a bowl add 4 Tbsp. of Glue to 5 Tbsps. of Corn Starch

Mix

Mix in dying agents, glitter, beads and scent until color and fragrance is to your liking.

Add 2 - 3 Teaspoons of Activator

Mix thoroughly and adjust activator until proper consistency is achieved.

Add ½ Tbsp. of Hand Lotion

Mix

Store in an airtight container

Clear Slime

This recipe produces a glass like slime that can be colored. Dyes allow for translucency while paint is deeper but less clear. Good for artistic projects.

Difficulty: Easy

Review: 4 / 5

Supplies:

Clear Glue

Water

Food Coloring / Dye (Optional)

Activator (See Solutions for Recipe)

Scenting Agent (Optional)

Glitter (Optional)

Directions: Makes 3 Ounces.

In a Bowl, add 4 tbsp. of Clear Glue with 2 tbsp. of Water.

Mix slowly using the drag technique.

Mix in dying agents, glitter, beads and scent until color and fragrance is to your liking.

Add approximately ½ - 2 tsp. of Activator. Adjust amount of activator until consistency is correct.

Mix thoroughly until proper consistency is achieved.

Pro Tip: The longer it sits the clearer it becomes.

Store in Airtight Container.

Green Clear Slime

Blue & Green Clear Slime

Limited
Edition

Red Slime
with Beads

Cream Cheese Slime

Slightly softer than a Butter Slime and doesn't require the addition of soft clay. An Excellent Slime to play with.

Difficulty: Hard

Review: 4.5 / 5

Supplies:

White or Clear Glue

Corn Starch

Foaming Hand Soap

Shaving Cream

Activator

Food Dye or Paint (optional)

Glitter (optional)

Scenting Agent (optional)

Directions:

Makes 3 Ounces

In a bowl add 3 Tbsp. of Glue to 3 Tbsp. of Corn Starch

Mix

Mix in 2 Tbsp. Foaming Hand Soap

Add 1 Tbsp. Shaving Cream

Mix thoroughly until proper consistency is achieved.

Mix in dying agents, glitter, beads and scent until color and fragrance is to your liking.

Add ½ - 1 Tsp Activator

Mix thoroughly and adjust activator until proper consistency is achieved.

Pro Tip: If slime is tight add ½ tbsp. of foaming soap

Store in an airtight container

Green Cream Cheese Swirl

Normal

Floam Slime

A clear slime with foam beads. It has a crunchy feel and sound.

Difficulty: Medium

Review: 3.5 / 5

Supplies:

Clear Glue

Water

Polystyrene Beads

Food Coloring / Dye (Optional)

Activator (See Solutions for Recipe)

Scenting Agent (Optional)

Glitter (Optional)

Directions:

Makes 3 Ounces.

In a Bowl, add 4 tbsp. of Clear Glue to 2 tbsp. of Water.

Mix

Mix in dying agents, glitter, and scent until color and fragrance is to your liking.

Add ½ to 1 tsp. of Activator. Adjust amount of activator until consistency is correct. You want a slightly stickier slime so that the beads will adhere so less activator is used than a normal slime.

Add beads into slime until desired consistency is achieved.

For a 1 to 1 Ratio:

Stretch slime and lower into a bowl until slime is coated in beads.

Knead.

Dip into beads again making sure to cover any exposed slime.

Knead

For a lower bead ratio:

Place slime in a bowl or container and spoon in beads until consistency is achieved

For more details see our video at www.studiopengu.com/slime

Pro Tip: Add various sizes and materials to create awesome effects

Store in Airtight Container.

Big Beads 1 to 1 Ratio   1 to ½ Ratio   1 to 1 Ratio

Limited Edition

Fluffy Slime

Clear glue creates a thicker slime that can be stretched to appear like glass whereas Colors tend to show up better when Clear Glue is used. White glue creates a slightly stretchier version and is generally less expensive.

Difficulty: Easy

Review: 4 / 5

Supplies:

White or Clear Glue

Shaving Cream

Hand Lotion

Activator (See Solutions for Recipe)

Food Coloring / Paint (Optional)

Scenting Agent (Optional)

Directions: Makes 2 ½ Ounces.

In a Bowl, mix 4 tbsp. of White Glue with 7 tbsp. of Shaving Cream.

Add 1/8 tbsp. of Lotion.

Mix.

Mix in dying agents, glitter, and scent until color and fragrance is to your liking.

Add ½ to 1 tsp. of Activator. Adjust amount of activator until consistency is correct.

Mix thoroughly until proper consistency is achieved.

Store in Airtight Container.

Frosting Slime

A good slime for projects. It gets its name from it ability to be spread and hold its shape.

Difficulty: Easy

Review: 4 / 5

Supplies:

White Glue

Shaving Cream

Hand Lotion

Activator (See Solutions for Recipe)

Corn Starch

Food Coloring / Paint (Optional)

Scenting Agent (Optional)

Directions: Makes 2 ½ Ounces.

In a Bowl, mix 4 tbsp. of White Glue with 7 tbsp. of Shaving Cream.

Mix in 1/8 tbsp. of Lotion.

Mix in dying agents, glitter, and scent until color and fragrance is to your liking.

Add ½ to 1 tsp. of Activator. Adjust amount of activator until consistency is correct.

Mix thoroughly until proper consistency is achieved.

Add 4 Tbsp. of Corn Starch to the slime and knead Thoroughly.

Store in Airtight Container.

Glossy Slime

A slime that feels like Fluffy Slime, but is more jelly-like. It has a Glossy finish.

Difficulty: Medium

Review: 4.5 / 5

Supplies:

White Glue

Baby Oil

Foaming Soap

Activator

Scenting Agent (optional)

Directions: Makes 2 Ounces

In a bowl add 4 Tbsp. of White Glue to ½ - 1 Tbsp. Baby Oil (the more oil the shinier the slime)

Mix

Mix in 2 Tbsp. of Foaming Hand Soap

Mix in dying agents, glitter, beads and scent until color and fragrance is to your liking.

Add 1-2 Teaspoons of Activator

Mix thoroughly and adjust activator until proper consistency is achieved.

Pro Tip: Let Sit for 2-3 for Glossy Effect to fully appear

Store in an airtight container

Jiggly Slime

Extremely sticky, Jiggly Slime is excellent for poking. It jiggles when you poke it.

Difficulty: Medium

Review: 3 / 5

Supplies:

Fluffy Slime (see recipe)

Water

Activator

Food Dye or Paint (optional)

Glitter (optional)

Scenting Agent (optional)

Directions: Makes 1 Ounce

In a bowl add 2 Tbsp. of Fluffy Slime to 6 Tbsp. of Water

Mix

Add in dying agents, glitter, etc. and scent until color and fragrance is to your liking.

Mix

Add ½ - 1 Tsp Activator

Mix thoroughly until proper consistency is achieved.

Pro Tip: Jiggly Slime can be turned into Oobleck Slime, a crafting slime.

Store in an airtight container

Marshmallow Slime

An exceptional slime for audio satisfaction. Not too stretchy. It produces lots of bubbles when left to sit.

Difficulty: Medium

Review: 5 / 5

Supplies:

White or Clear Glue

Foaming Hand Soap

Shaving Cream

Corn Starch

Corn Starch

Activator

Food Dye or Paint (optional)

Glitter (optional)

Scenting Agent (optional)

Directions:

Makes 3 1/2 Ounces

In a bowl add 4 Tbsp. of Glue to 3 Tbsp. of Foaming Hand Soap

Mix

Add 4 Tbsp. Shaving Cream

Mix

Add 3 Tbsp. of Corn Starch

Mix

Add in dying agents, glitter, beads and scent until color and fragrance is to your liking.

Mix

Add 1-2 Tsp Activator

Mix thoroughly until proper consistency is achieved.

Add ½ Tsp Foaming Hand Soap

Mix

Store in an airtight container

Rainbow Marshmallow Slime

Normal

Oobleck Slime

An interesting slime that holds its shape for a brief second before turning into an ooze that can be used to cover objects.

Difficulty: Hard

Review: 4 / 5

Supplies:

Fluffy Slime (Scent and dye before starting). (See recipe for details)

Water

Corn Starch

Activator

Directions: Makes 1 Ounce

In a bowl add 2 Tbsp. of Fluffy Slime to 6 Tbsp. of Corn Starch

Mix

Add ½ to 1 tsp. of Activator. Adjust amount of activator until consistency is correct.

Mix in 4 Tbsp. of Corn Starch

Pro Tip: Pour over a soda can and let harden for a unique piece of art.

Store in an airtight container

Pearl Slime

Our version doesn't require the addition of expensive pigments.

Difficulty: Medium

Review: 4 / 5

Supplies:

Clear Glue

Water Shaving Cream

Activator

Pearlizer (See recipe below)

Food Coloring / Dye (Optional)

Scenting Agent (Optional)

Glitter (Optional)

Directions:

Makes 3 Ounces.

In a Bowl, add 4 tbsp. of Clear Glue with 2 tbsp. of Pearlizer. (Recipe below)

Mix slowly using the drag technique.

Add in dying agents, glitter, beads and scent until color and fragrance is to your liking.

Mix

Mix in approximately ½ - 2 tsp. of Activator. Adjust amount of activator until consistency is correct.

Pro Tip: The longer it sits the more prominent the pearl effect becomes.

Store in Airtight Container.

Pearlizer

Add 5 Tbsp. of Shaving Cream to 1 Cup of Water.

Mix thoroughly

Pour into a bottle or container and let sit for a few minutes to allow solids to dissolve.

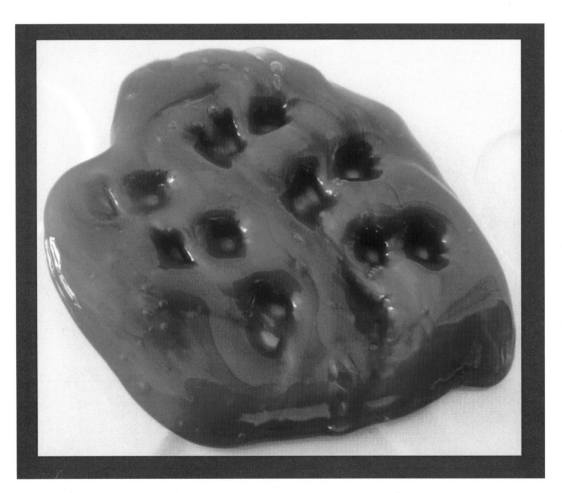

Green Pearl Slime

Limited Edition

Quick Clear Slime

A visual slime, great for adding beads and glitter to.

Difficulty: Easy

Review: 3 / 5

Supplies:

Clear Glue

Water

Activator

Glitter (optional)

Beads (optional)

Foam Beads (optional)

Small Toys (optional)

Directions: Makes 2 1/2 Ounces

In a bowl add 2 Tbsp. of Clear Glue to 4 Tbsp. of Water

Mix slowly using the drag technique.

Add 1-2 Teaspoons of Activator

Mix thoroughly and adjust activator until proper consistency is achieved.

Add in dying agents, glitter, beads, small toys and scent until color and fragrance is to your liking.

Pro Tip: Add more water to make the Slime clear up faster

Store in an airtight container

Soft Serve Slime

It has a consistency like soft serve ice cream. A fun slime to play around with and awesome for swirling.

Difficulty: Medium

Review: 4 / 5

Supplies:

White or Clear Glue

Shaving Cream

Foaming Hand Soap

Baby Oil

Corn Starch

Hand Lotion

Activator

Food Dye or Paint (optional)

Glitter (optional)

Scenting Agent (optional)

Directions: Makes 3 Ounces

In a bowl add 4 Tbsp. of Glue to 3 Tbsp. of Foaming Hand Soap

Mix

Add 3 Tbsp. Hand Lotion

Mix

Add ½ Tbsp. Baby Oil

Mix

Add in 2 Tbsp. Corn Starch

Mix thoroughly

Add 1 Tbsp. Shaving Cream

Mix

Add in dying agents, glitter, beads and scent until color and fragrance is to your liking.

Mix

Add 1-2 Tsp Activator

Mix thoroughly and adjust activator until proper consistency is achieved.

Knead in 1 Tbsp. Corn Starch

Store in an airtight container

Soft-Serve Slime

Normal

Sonic Slime

A super stretchy slime with a good high pitch sound for squishing.

Difficulty: Medium

Review: 4 / 5

Supplies:

White or Clear Glue

Shaving Cream

Hand Lotion

Foaming Hand Soap

Activator

Food Dye or Paint (optional)

Glitter (optional)

Scenting Agent (optional)

Directions:

Makes 4 Ounces

In a bowl add 4 Tbsp. of Glue to 1 Tbsp. of Shaving Cream

Mix

Add 3 Tbsp. Hand Lotion

Mix

Add 2 Tbsp. Foaming Hand Soap

Mix

Add in Scents, Glitter etc.

Mix

Add 2-4 Tsp Activator

Mix thoroughly until proper consistency is achieved.

Store in an airtight container

To Make the Sonic Boom Variant

This slime feels like sonic slime. Makes a deeper sound.

Difficulty: Medium

Review: 4 / 5

Using the previous recipe make a batch of Sonic Slime

Knead in 2 Tbsp. Corn Starch

Add ½ Teaspoons of Activator

Mix thoroughly until proper consistency is achieved.

Pro Tip: The sounds are more pronounced when slime is in a plastic soufflé cup.

Store in an airtight container

Galaxy Slime

Limited
Edition

Spa Slime

Spa Slime soothes dry hands in a funny way.

Difficulty: Easy

Review: 4 / 5

Supplies:

White Glue

Shaving Cream

Hand Lotion

Activator (See Solutions for Recipe)

Food Coloring / Paint (Optional)

Scenting Agent (Optional)

Directions:

Makes 2 ½ Ounces.

In a Bowl, add 4 tbsp. of White Glue to 2 tbsp. of Hand Lotion

Mix slightly.

Add 1 tbsp. of Shaving Cream.

Mix.

Mix in dying agents, glitter, and scent until color and fragrance is to your liking.

Add 1 to 3 tsp. of Activator.

Do Not Mix

Add 2 Tbsp. of Lotion

Add 1 Tbsp. of Shaving Cream

Mix and Knead together

Adjust amount of activator until consistency is correct.

Pro Tip: Add scents to convey a calming or energizing mood, such as Lavender or Lemon.

Store in Airtight Container.

Lemon Drop Floam
on Rainbow
Background

Normal

Taiko Slime

Named for the Japanese Drum, this slime produces deep bass noise when thumped.

Difficulty: Easy

Review: 4.5 / 5

Supplies:

Clear Glue

Water

Activator

Glitter (optional)

Beads or Small Toys (optional)

Directions: Makes 2 1/2 Ounces

In a bowl add 4 Tbsp. of Clear Glue to 4 Tbsp. of Water

Mix slowly using the drag technique.

Add in dying agents, glitter, beads and scent until color and fragrance is to your liking.

Add 2 - 3 Teaspoons of Activator

Mix thoroughly and adjust activator until proper consistency is achieved.

Pro Tip: The sounds are more pronounced when slime is in a plastic soufflé cup.

Store in an airtight container

Therapeutic Slime

This slime is great for relaxation or exercising. Cab be used rehab tired or sore hands. Adding a scenting agent can increase the therapeutic quality of this slime. Lemon or Mint Scent creates an energizing aroma. Lavender Oil creates a relaxing scent while Bubblegum Scents can make it more playful.

Difficulty: Easy

Review: 4 / 5

Supplies:

White Glue

Corn Starch

Hand Lotion

Activator

Scenting Agent (optional)

Directions:

Makes 4 Ounces

In a bowl, add 4 Tbsp. of White Glue to 2 Tbsp. of Corn Starch (Makes Soft Version. See Chart Below to Adjust Firmness)

Mix

Add in 1 Tbsp. of Hand Lotion

Mix

Add in dying agents and / or scent until color and fragrance is to your liking.

Mix

Add 2-3 Teaspoons of Activator

Mix thoroughly and adjust activator until proper consistency is achieved.

Firmness Chart

2 Tbsp. Corn Starch = Soft

3 Tbsp. Corn Starch = Medium

4 Tbsp. Corn Starch = Firm

5-6 Tbsp. Corn Starch = Extra Firm

Oils and their Effect

1. Mint – Energizing
2. Lavender – Calming and Relaxing. Great before sleep
3. Lemon – Promotes mental clarity
4. Rose- Balance and Harmony
5. Orange – Uplifting
6. Citrus (Grapefruit, Lime) – Uplifting
7. Jasmine - Tranquility

Pro Tip: Use hand lotion on hands before using for a deep moisture treatment.

Store in an airtight container

Therapeutic Slime ready for use

Projects

Normal

Avalanche Slime

Avalanche Slime is a mixture of Fluffy and Clear Slime that creates amazing color combinations.

Place a ball of clear slime at the bottom of a jar or soufflé cup. Place an equal amount of Fluffy Slime on top of the Clear Slime. White fluffy works the best.

Left upright it will form Stalactites.

If tilted on side it gives more of an octopus effect.

Avalanche Slime Avalanching

Limited
Edition

Glow-in-the-Dark

Slime can be made to Glow-in-the-Dark by using paints that have Glow-in-the-Dark Pigments added to it. Make sure to use a water based acrylic paint.

Whatever color you choose it will dye the slime that color. To make a Clear Glow-in-the-Dark Slime use a Glow-in-the-Dark Finish Paint. Mix with the water before adding glue to keep the opaqueness.

Chameleon / Color Changing Slime

By using Thermochromic Pigments, you can create a slime that changes color when heat or cold are applied. For example, if you add red pigments to a blue slime when the temperature change happens, you will have a purple slime.

There are many colors and temperatures available. Make sure you get a temperature suitable for your area or put the slime in the freezer for a few minutes.

It can be added to any slime.

Mix in ½ to 1 Teaspoon of pigment to most recipes

When slime is cold use warm tools, metal letters or even your hand.

When slime is warm, place tools, letters etc. in the freezer or use ice.

Chameleon Slime

Normal

Holiday Themed Slimes

Themed slimes are a cool way to celebrate the holiday or occasion.

New Year's Eve: Black Slime with holographic glitter or Clear Slime in champagne flutes

Chinese Day Years: Red Fluffy Slime with Gold glitter

Valentines: Use red and pinks or make heart shaped Floams

Birthday Slime – Use pastel colored Frosting slime with colored beads. You can also make Butter or Clay Slime and build a birthday cake. In our project section, we make a party slime called Robot Slime.

St Patrick's Day: Add green glitter to Green Clear Slime.

Normal

Easter: Make Jiggly Slime with pastel and neon colors and place in plastic eggs.

Mother's Day: Make Pink Spa Slime with plastic diamond shaped beads.

Memorial Day / Fourth of July: Make red white and blue avalanche slimes.
To Make: Place Red and Blue Clear Slime with White Fluffy Slime on top and let sit.

Halloween: Use Black and Orange Clay Slime to make Jack O Lanterns. Or create Glow-in-the-Dark Slimes to decorate, give out or to act as party place holders.

Normal

Thanksgiving: Use Yellow, Orange and Brown Slimes to create a rainbow or an avalanche. Decorate with stickers and use as an interesting place card.

Christmas:

Add Red, Silver, and / or Green glitter to slimes.

Place large foam beads into Red Clear Slime to create a holiday themed centerpiece.

Party Favor Slime

This is a great party favor / place card for birthday parties.

Any slime and plastic toy will work but to create a slime that won't stick to toy, thoroughly mix equal parts of Clear and Fluffy Slime. This will create a fun stretchy slime that won't stick.

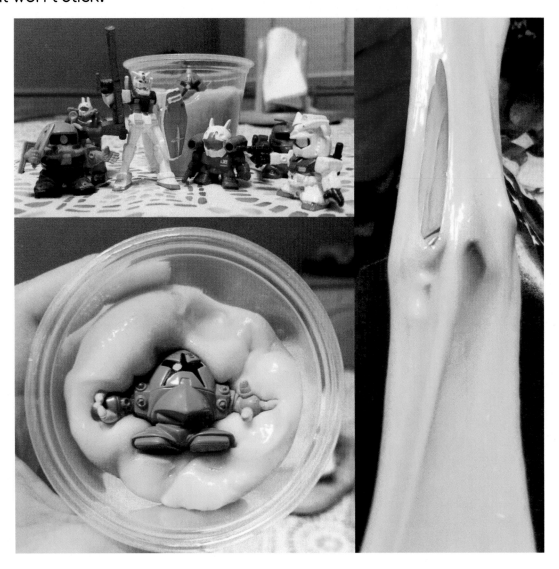

Decorate 5 Ounce Soufflé Cups

Write guests name on lid.

Fill with Slime Mixture.

Press a plastic toy into slime and allow to sink overnight.

Toy Ideas:

Plastic Dinosaurs, Robot, Pokémon Figures, Animals such as Dogs or Horses

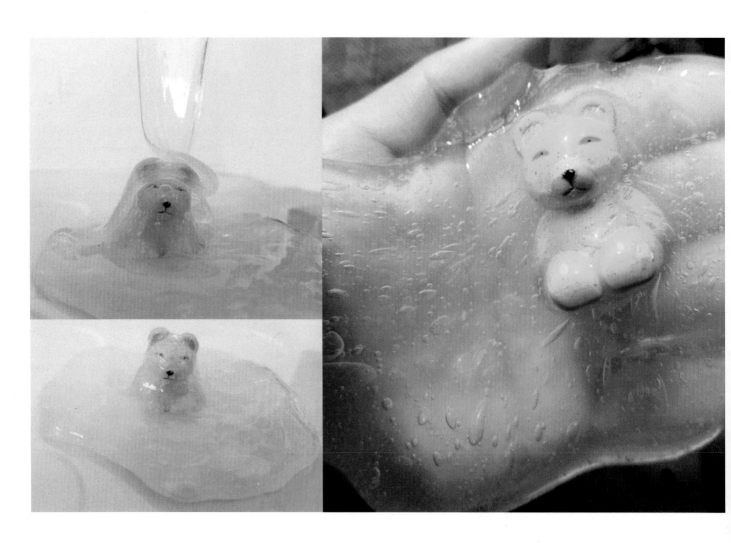

Normal

Mermaid Slime

This fun shimmering slime is great for girl's parties.

To Make:

Start by making a Green Clear Slime and a Blue Clear Slime.

In a cup mix 3 Parts of Green to 1 Part of Blue.

Once blended add in lots of holographic glitter.

Mermaid Slime

Molten Lava Chocolate Cake

Our version features a chocolate cake filled with gooey 'Orange Cream Lava.'

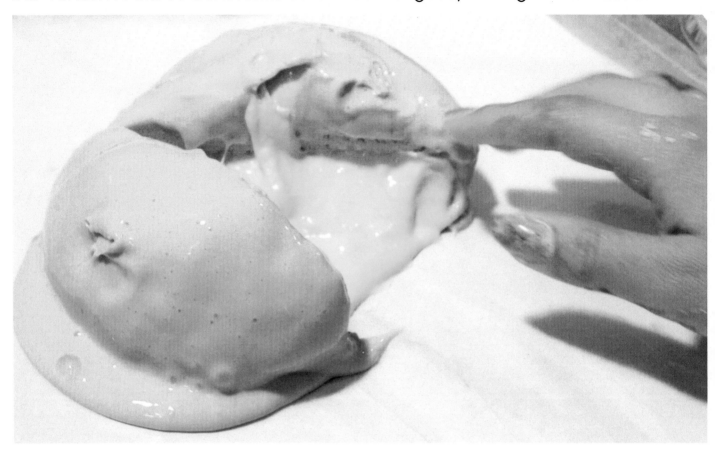

Supplies

12 Ounces of White Butter Slime

7 Ounces of Oobleck Slime

Brown Acrylic Paint

Orange Acrylic Paint

Large Coffee Mug

Wax Paper

Rolling Pin

Large Circular Cookie Cutter

Knife

Directions:

Seasonal

Begin by adding the brown paint to the Butter Slime and mixing until paint is completely worked in.

Roll the Butter Slime into a cylinder.

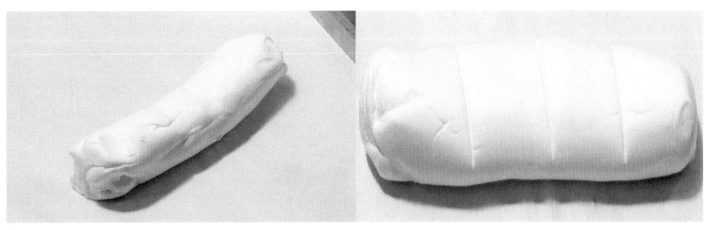

Mark the cylinder into eighths.

Cut off 5/8 for cake. Save the rest for the lid.

Place a sheet of wax paper over the coffee mug mouth and gently press it in.

Roll the 5/8 section into a ball

Place the section in the mug mouth and push towards the bottom. As it goes in pull the slime up the walls of the mug to form a crater.

Take the remaining brown slime and roll flat using fresh wax paper.

Keep this layer somewhat thick

Once flat, remove the top layer of wax paper.

Using the Cookie Cutter, cut out a circle.

If needed, roll circle until it is large enough to cover top of cake. You need it overlap the mug mouth so leave an inch or so.

Pour Oobleck Slime into the cup until it reaches the top.

Place the circle of Brown Slime over the top and pinch around the edges to seal.

Flip the mug upside down onto a piece of wax paper and remove the cake.

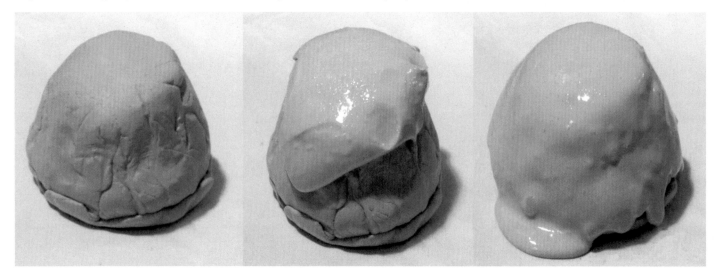

Roll the Brown Oobleck into a ball and place it on top of cake.

Let the Oobleck cover the cake.

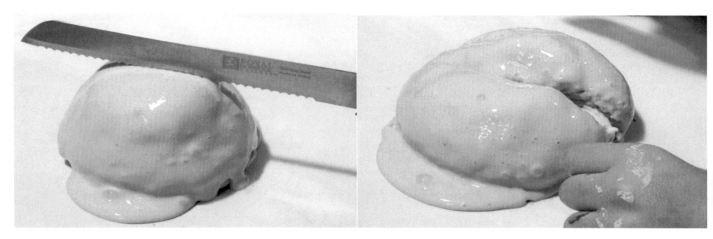

Slice open to reveal the lava…but do not eat.

Battenberg Cake

This project is based on a Battenberg Cake, an English Cake of alternating yellow and pink sponge cakes held together with apricot jam and covered in marzipan.

When made in a similar fashion but with different flavors or colors it is called a checkerboard or domino cake.

Supplies

15 Ounces of White Butter Slime

Red Food Coloring

Yellow Food Coloring

Wax Paper

Rolling Pin

Pizza Cutter

Knife

Directions:

Roll into a cylinder

Divide in half.

Divide one half in half. Each of these halves will be used for the cake.

Take the other half and remove a third. The large portion will be used for the marzipan and the small portion for decorations.

Take the half for the cake and divide into fourths.

Dye 2 of the fourths pink and 2 of them yellow.

Form each section into a rectangle.

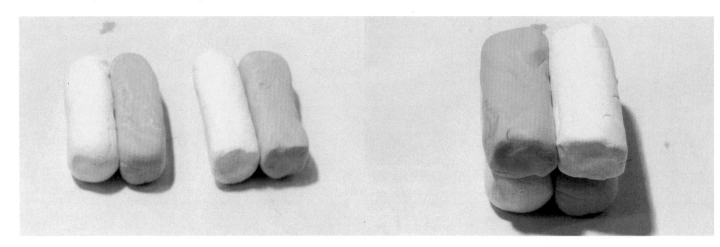

Stack a yellow on top of a pink section and reverse for the last 2.

Take the section reserved for the marzipan and place onto a sheet of wax paper. Place another sheet of wax paper on top and roll out until it is twice as big as the stack.

Using the pizza cutter trim the slime until it is a rectangle.

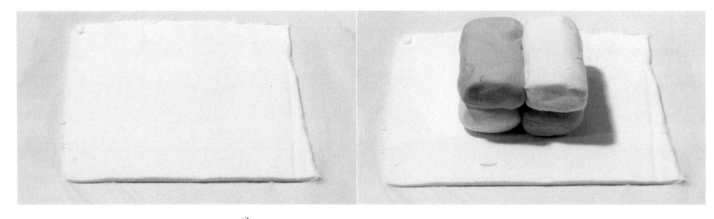

Once the marzipan is rolled out, place the stack of cakes on top and gently fold up the edges and then the ends.

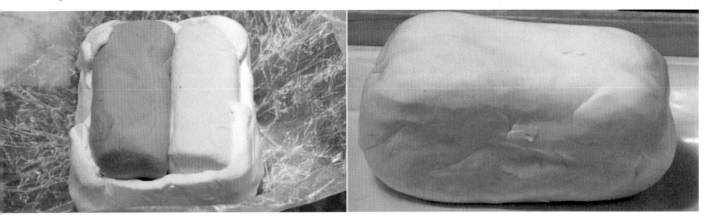

The remaining slime will be used to decorate the top of the cake. It can be left white or dyed pink or yellow. Use this slime to form dollops, roses etc. and stick on top of the cake.

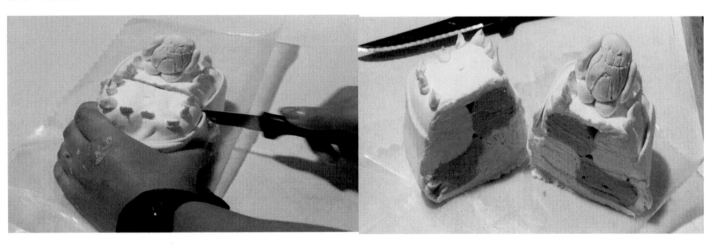

Special

Things to do with your Slime

1. Balloons – Put some slime on the end of a straw and blow into the straw, Bubble Blowing Slime is best. See our video at www.studiopengu.com/slime

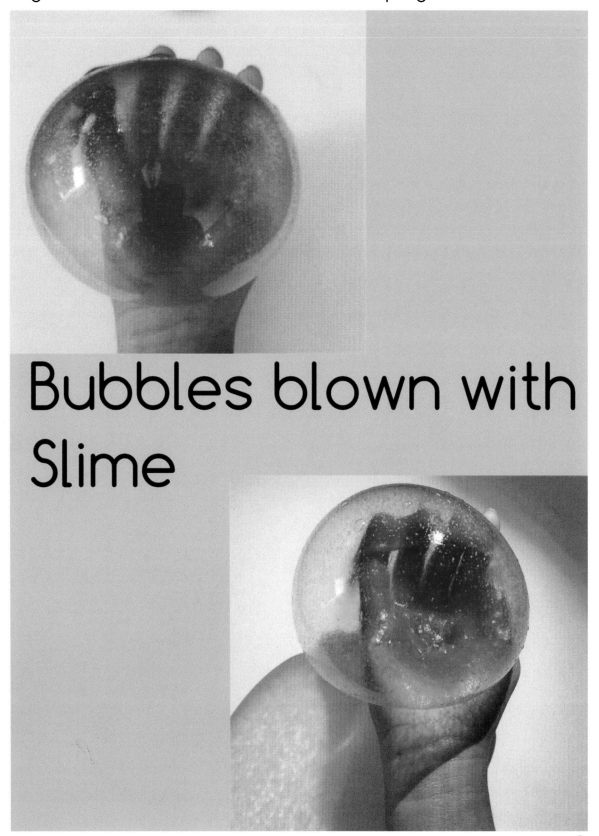

Bubbles blown with Slime

Limited Edition

2. Bubbles – Let any slime sit untouched for 2+ days to form bubbles on top

3. Spinning on Drill – If have a drill, put some slime on the drill bit and start spinning it! Use a box to contain the slime and allow it to mix into random shapes. Make sure to have an adult nearby and always be careful!
See our video at www.studiopengu.com/slime

4. Crackling Bubbles – Take some slime and pull a corner on top of the slime. Continue folding it over from different slides until you want to squeeze it. You will instantly get awesome crackling sounds!

5. Dried Art – Let some random slime dry on cool items to get awesome effects! You can also try to remove it from the surface to get great sculptures.

Slime Bird created by spinning slimes on Cordless Drill

Dried Shapes

Oobleck over Dried Fluffy Slime

Form shapes as slime begins to harden.

For ease of removal place on wax paper.

Purple Fluffy poured over Cup & Can

Slime First Aid

If store properly slimes can last several months or more. Climate and other factors can lead to slimes losing some their properties. Color and scents can be augmented over time by adding more of same. while other issues take more effort

1. Hardening Slime – if a slime is losing its ability to stretch take the following steps, depending on type of slime

   Non- Clear Slimes – Knead in Hand Lotion or Shaving Cream until consistency returns to normal

   Clear Slimes – Briefly soak in warm water and knead in. Do Not Use too much water or leave in water for too long or it will dissolve slime

2. Loss of Fluffiness – For non- clear slimes add shaving cream to return Fluff.

3. Overly Sticky – For all slimes adding a bit of activator will take the stickiness out of your slime

4. Melted – Put in freezer for 30 minutes. You may need to take other steps to remedy other issues that arise when slime melts such as adding activator.

5. Frozen – Let thaw in the refrigerator You may need to take other steps to remedy other issues that arise when slime is frozen such as adding Lotion to reactivate the stretchy properties.

Meet the Authors

Based in Southern California, Studio Pengu is a creative house that produces multimedia presentations and projects. We operate several online stores, a YouTube channel and several Instagram and Snap Chat Accounts.

Izzy aka Isabella is the master chef. At the age of 11 she already earns money creating slimes and selling them online. She is the creative mind of the operation

Dan aka Daniel has been writing for over 30 Years. His works have been featured in corporate ads and newspapers. He is the grunt of the operation.

Aimee aka Mom is the backbone of the operations. From supply acquisition to balancing the checkbook, Aimee is a behind the scenes workhouse. She is clearly the brains of the operation.

Duke and Dutch aka the world's greatest dogs are both rescue dogs who appear in our videos whether invited or not. They are the Cuteness of the Operation.

Thank You from the bottom of our hearts for purchasing this book. We hope you enjoy it.